Celebrate Your Emotions

A Guide to Eight Incredibly Transforming Feelings

Celebrate Your Emotions:
A Guide to Eight Incredibly Transforming Feelings

 Published by Relationship Publications™

Printed in the United States of America
ISBN: 1-4392-3113-3

Dedicated to Nancy, Alex, Jessica, Marissa, Ken and Orange:
Thank you for helping me to do better.

Celebrate Your Emotions:

A Guide to Eight Incredibly Transforming Feelings

Introduction

Emotions are what put us in tune with one another, our fellow creatures, and earth itself. The problem is that we are too often either tuned out of our emotions...or overly tuned in and overwhelmed by them. Either way, we don't use them effectively.

The solution is to learn what emotions really mean and how to use them in counterpoint to words and deeds. We need to understand and befriend emotions as the helpers they are meant to be in shaping our lives for the better.

People think thousands of thoughts a day, often repetitively and without gaining self-knowledge and improving their lives.

Mind control and positive thinking often fall far short of tapping your full potential for happiness. You need to spend more time feeling, and understanding the meaning of your feelings to put you in the "now", and to reduce pointless or compulsive over-thinking.

Negative emotions just mean that you have unsolved problems. Once you admit and understand a negative emotion you have a much better shot at solving the problems associated with it. When you solve any part of any problem you automatically experience joy. Even if you fail to notice it.

"Bad" thoughts don't just cause problems. They are also valuable clues to emotional problems and potential cures. If you suppress a bad thought, you also suppress the emotional information associated with it. That impairs growth. It also increases the probability that you will be ambushed later by the emotions you just suppressed.

Far better to figure out the emotions represented by your "bad" thoughts. Then you can both think and feel your way into better thoughts.

All the positive thinking in the world cannot overcome the simple reality that emotions rule even more than logic.

In my clinical work with young children, I have been dazzled to see the speed of their recovery simply from having their emotional expressions understood and "talked to" with emotion in return. Transferring play techniques to adults, I have been cheered by increased patient/client freedom in dealing with issues.

I have so much enthusiasm for the power and wisdom of emotions that I sometimes feel like a zealous public relations agent when I talk or write about them.

But truly, the payoffs are numerous and cumulative. You will develop more of a personality: your own, special, unique and caring personality, less encumbered by conditioning. That will help free you to find and follow your true passions in life. Following your true passion is a moral and spiritual issue for all of us.

Each of us must evolve. The time is now. As a public relations agent for the emotions, I earnestly hope that you will enjoy and grow from this short book.

[For clients'/patients' confidentiality, case examples do not use real names, and identifying information has been changed.]

CHAPTER I

Body Language, Body Movement, and Play

Dr. Sharon Says

For your mind to fully know it
let your body physically show it.

All sensation is both
physical in movement and emotional in meaning.

Watch your way through thinking
and move your way through feeling.

We have two categories of language

- **Thoughts:** words and images.
- **Feelings:** sensations and movements... emotions.

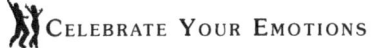

We have to take turns listening to our minds, and our bodies

- Just as you think constantly, your body speaks to you constantly, telling you nonstop things about yourself and the world around you that words or even pictures alone can't convey.

- You cannot consciously think two thoughts at the same time. Try it. Similarly you cannot consciously think a thought and feel a feeling at the same time. That's because your mind has to be quiet in order to observe something like a feeling.

- You literally have to take turns between thinking and feeling. Many times you do this rapidly, automatically. Many times you don't. You have to detour away from your thinking, at times, to make time to feel.

Learn to play with your feelings

- Act them out and use them alternating with your words.

    o   Words alone leave information cluttered and clouded so you can't use it to the best.

    o   Stop thinking the same thoughts by learning to move your body with the feelings associated with them. Then you can get on your way to new and improved thoughts.

    o   Moving with your feelings helps send your entire unconscious mind to work on your problem or opportunity.

New moves in life come more easily when you let yourself move emotionally.

Words are partial translations of feelings. Playful movement with your feelings says the rest

- Playing with your emotions gets them out into the light of day where you can realize them, understand them better and respond to them with better results.

- Without play, you can easily deceive yourself into thinking that you are "over" various difficulties even though there are unsolved parts.

- Without play, you can easily miss prejudices and limitations of attitudes and beliefs.

Incredibly Transforming Feelings – The Eight Super-Transformers

Over the years, eight feelings have emerged as pivotal in managing all other thoughts and feelings. I call them "super transformers" because they galvanize change in regular, positive, and predictable ways. One patient described this aspect of treatment as "a way to feel the feeling in its pure form. All must be experienced to the fullest for them to make room for the next feeling. Otherwise it leaves a residue."

- **Joy:** Marks rightness of event or action. Spreads a sense of fulfillment, freedom and power—felt as a jumping sensation, from perineal/pubic areas on up or lifting you off your feet and urge to throw your arms up in "V" of victory.

- **Ambivalence:** Keeps your head and heart "talking" with each other—felt as tension or restlessness in neck and shoulders.

- **Hostility:** Discloses power and information in dangerous, explosive forms—felt as stress, pressure, tension in
your body, or explosive urge to blame.

- **Pain:** Draws in help needed to solve a problem—felt as
stomach pain, general physical pain, tension of resisting,
or yawning.

- **Hate:** Helps get rid of unhealthy patterns of behavior—
felt as yucky taste or nauseous feeling.

- **Confusion:** Disrupts dead-end thinking and energizes
for creating new and improved thinking—felt as fore-
head level pressure or even headache.

- **Shame:** Presses you out of "improper" behavior toward
better behavior—felt as hiding or wish to hide.

- **Laughter:** Catapults you out of chaos into understanding and out of agony into ecstasy. Through fear and pain
and into joy. Felt as bubbling or upwardly moving internal tickling.

Physical and Mental Exercise

Purpose: To show yourself how important your feelings are.

- How do you show happiness? Use both facial and body
movement and positions … no words or sounds.

- Now without any facial or body expression, say, "I am
Happy."

- Which feels more real? Expression with feeling, even
when you don't utter a sound!

Continued

Purpose: Learn more about yourself.

- Think of an emotion you don't like such as shame, hostility or pain.

- Now try to act out this disliked emotion without words or sounds.

- Write down the thoughts and feelings you have and keep them for exploration and change as you read through this book.

Mental and Spiritual Exercise

Step #1: Write on a note card: "I feel more alive when I take time to feel." Read it first out loud, then murmuring the words under your breath, and lastly silently. Do this immediately upon awakening and before bed at night for 21 days.

Step #2: Write a note: "I intend to learn more from my emotions than I ever thought possible." Place it on a frequently seen surface like your desk, computer monitor, medicine cabinet.

Remember

To "listen" to your body and to appreciate the importance of learning how to interpret its signals. Eight especially transformative emotions and their physical language have been introduced along with their benefits. The information and exercises about valuing and paying better attention to certain feelings can lead you to feel more alive and authentic.

Celebrate !!

❊ Feeling freer to be yourself.

❊ Being more able to recognize problematic contradictions in your own thoughts and feelings.

❊ Finding that you can follow through better on your intentions.

❊ Becoming more savvy to what others around you are "saying" in word, deed and feeling.

CHAPTER 2

Joy Is Enlightening

Dr. Sharon Says

Prevent hip replacement.
Wiggle with excitement. Jump for joy.

The enlightenment of joy can illuminate
any opportunity and every challenge.

To enjoy joy is a moral responsibility
and social opportunity.

Joy completes **EVERY** full cycle of emotion

- Joy only requires expression.
- Pain is meant to lead to repair, and joy.
- Fear is meant to resolve in the joy of safety.
- Anger is meant to cause constructive action, resulting in joy.
- By simply celebrating joy, you spread light, radiate well-being.
- Expressing joy helps lead to further en-light-enment.

Everyone's life is filled with joy, much of it unnoticed

- **Joy is ignored**: When things are nerve-wracking, stressful, annoying or tragic, the tendency is to notice only the negative and to forget the positive.

- **Joy is forgotten**: In the busyness and preoccupation that we problem-solving humans have, it's all too easy to notice only the problems needing solving. There is joy to be experienced from each part solved, every step of the way. By adulthood it's on to the next project, on to the next chore, and the weight of unfinished business casts long dark shadows over personal joy.

- **Did you know**: Joy is a concentration of sensation that occurs in your perineal area. It's therefore easily confused with sexuality and easily repressed and rejected for that reason.

  o **Only a century ago** women weren't allowed unseemly expression of happiness (sway), excitement (wiggle) or joy (jump).

  o **Only 50 years ago** it was up to women to keep their legs crossed and say "no" with no burden on the male if this system failed. Even now, in many parts of the country and the world, women's apparel is blamed for male come-ons. No wonder many women have lost their wiggle of excitement and their jump of joy.

o **In the process** men have similarly lost their wiggle. After all, if a man's wiggle and jump doesn't visibly put a happy wiggle and jump into his woman, then what good is it? When she can't show her pleasure in him with an excited wiggle and a joyful jump, how does he know he's really done the job right?

- **Commit to noticing your joy, feeling your joy, and expressing your joy**: It's too easy to miss it in the midst of emotions calling for further problem solving. It's too easy to miss it in the face of cultural attitudes suppressing it.

Physical Exercise

Purpose: To help you to feel your joy more fully

Step #1: Tune in

- Perineal/pubic Sensation: Any tingle or lightness in your perineal area is a signal of pure joy wanting expression. Any twitch, tension, pain or heaviness in the same area and/or your pubic area is a signal of joy long ignored. Check out your perineal/pubic feeling often without assuming it's about sex.

- Upward Lightness/Tingling Sensation: Feeling a sense of jumping, leaping, or elevating in any way is joy, including raising your hands above your head in the "V" of victory.

Step #2: Take off
In response to either perineal/pubic sensation, or general upward lightness/tingling sensations,

Continued

Physical Exercise, continued

- Stretch up tall and light, as if you are lifted off the ground by a surge of joy.

- Practice the "V" of victory using your arms. Mentally invite joy to check in with you more often.

- Vividly imagine jumping for joy. Imagine doing it as a kid and not getting in trouble for it. Imagine others joyfully acting out and celebrating your joy.

❖ STORY: Sexuality

Suzanne had difficulty feeling aroused by her husband, whom she loved very much. "I like to be touched by him, I love cuddling, but then when it comes to intercourse I suddenly seem to go dead." As she looked back on her sexual development, she remembered how her brothers had made cruel fun of her when she reached puberty. They joked about how her breasts bobbed around when she ran, and they went out of their way to act disgusted when they found any evidence of her menstrual periods. Putting that history of humiliation together with her current difficulty, Suzanne mused, "Sometimes when I make love with my husband, I cry. Now, it feels like I sort of know why."

Treatment

Suzanne was encouraged to view her crying as tears of joy (i.e., surging of joy over release of long pent-up pain). Instead of focusing on her tendency to "go dead" (her unconscious reliving the frozen humiliation she received from her brothers), she focused on the joy of being with her husband. Suzanne physically practiced joy...

○ *When she thought of her husband.*

- When she compared her husband's respect for her with her brothers' disrespect.

- In response to thoughts of sex with her husband.

- In the middle of enjoying his cuddles and caresses.

- When she felt "dead" during intercourse, knowing that her numbness was close to pain, and gain.

❖ STORY: A new phase in her sexuality

Suzanne was shocked at herself when she began behaving more seductively with her husband. "I actually guided his hand to you-know-where the other evening when we were standing around the kitchen. He loved it! We both did joy then." Similarly, she was amazed to find herself fantasizing about her husband, and began to love the adventure of flirtation with him. "Do you suppose I'm going through trying on sexuality, even in immature ways, like re-doing my teenage years?" So it seemed. With joy.

Spiritual Exercise

Purpose: To open yourself to practice of joy in both good and bad moments.

Step #1: Celebrate!

- Bring to mind something that made you happy or filled you with love. Think "Joy!"

- Bring to mind something that isn't yet right for you. Act out the feeling of "Joy!" that you are able to notice the problem, and "Joy!" that you care about the problem.

Continued

Step #2: Spread your joy.

- Regularly in your day rejoice in the beauty around you, the gifts in your life and the areas in which you are healthy.

- Pray a sentence or two often each day in gratitude for joy to God, Nature, The Cosmos, or those you love or care for.

- Once a week, write out some of your rejoicing or praise for good things or gratitude for joy in a Journal of Joy.

- Say your gratitude for your feelings of joy or say "Yay!!!" or other vocalization in expression of rejoicing out loud, whether for yourself alone or others to hear adding on a "Yay!!" or other joyful vocalization.

❖ STORY: Betrayal And Loss

Marie had recently been told by her husband that he had been having an affair for the past five years. They tried couples therapy, but he soon chose the other woman. Marie was devastated. Her life had been wrapped around her husband, they had been devoted friends and business partners, and she was completely blind-sided by his betrayal. Yet, away from psychological treatment, Marie found no place for her grief over losing her husband. Her friends said, "Why are you crying over him? He cheated on you for years, and now he's leaving you! What an asshole!"

Treatment

But Marie needed to cry. During one session in particular she did so at length. Sobbing, grieving at the betrayal by her husband, grieving at the loss, grieving at her loneliness.

- *Suddenly she said "I feel dizzy!" "That's happiness," I said, "Sway, smile."*

- She did so, and then said "I'm seeing spots before my eyes...!" "That's confetti," I said, "Joy!"
- She raised her arms up in the "V" for victory of joy.
- The light-headedness and spots before her eyes gradually subsided.

Relief at last

"I feel joyful to at last be able to cry," she said. "No one else would let me. I so needed to get it out." The surge of joy lasted about a minute, and then it was on to peeling back the next layer of her sadness. The joy helped Marie to fully appreciate her sadness and pain, and to allow it to "talk" to her. In the coming weeks, Marie was amazed to find that she was functioning well at work, but that when she would get in the car, she would begin to cry. She would cry off and on all evening until she went to sleep. She would sleep well and function well all the next day until it was time to drive home, when the crying would come again, allowed by joy.

Remember

This chapter explains how the super-transforming emotion of joy is easily and widely overlooked and suppressed. The information, exercises and case examples can help you increase both your sense of well-being and your ability to grow and spread the joy in your life.

Celebrate !!

✳ Feeling better because you can feel your joy better.

✳ Being able to accept your joys in the midst of sorrows.

✳ Finding that you are better able to see the opportunities in problems.

✳ Letting your sexuality grow in vitality and passion.

CHAPTER 3

Every Decision Requires Opposing Attitudes or Feelings

Dr. Sharon Says

Ambivalence is resistance
is a good thing.

Exercise your ambivalence to feel
and think your way through choices.

Ambivalence keeps your
head and heart talking.

The neck and shoulder tension
of ambivalence won't make you DO anything.

Opposing Thoughts and Feelings = Ambivalence

You are ambivalent when you are drawn and pushing toward action, but also pulled back and not wanting to take action.

- You sort of want to do something and sort of don't. Or you're sort of interested in something and sort of not.

- Your jaw, neck, and shoulders feel in conflict, some muscles pushing you toward something while other muscles try to pull you away.

Ambivalence Is Natural

In the realm of emotions and what to do about them, everyone is ambivalent (even professional psychologists). Just think of the contradictions you've heard.

- "Anger is bad." "Anger is healthy." "Crying is good." "Don't cry." "Don't hate so-and-so." "I hate him/her/them!" "You should be ashamed." "Don't be ashamed." "Laughter is healing." "Shame on you for laughing at her/him/that!"

- All ambivalence involves differences between what your head thinks and how your heart feels. You think you should do something, but you don't feel like it. You really want to do something, but you think you shouldn't.

Feeling both sides of anything improves decision-making

- The very nature of a decision requires ambivalence: opposing thoughts and feelings.

- Mentally confronting contradictions in habits you've believed unchangeable—anything from procrastination to drug/alcohol abuse, from a short fuse to chronic doormat behavior—and pairing your thoughts and feelings with the physical movements of ambivalence will automatically begin to move you out of stagnation.

Staying in touch with ambivalence keeps your head and heart talking to each other

❖ STORY: Weight Loss-Gain

Liz began treatment because she was tired of carrying a lot of body fat. She thought that she was held back from gaining control over her diet because her fat was so important in protecting her from unwanted sexual attention. She was scared to let go of the protection it offered. She wanted to get rid of her "garbage" that was intertwined with her weight, but she also despaired at times and just didn't want to try any more.

Treatment

- *When Liz was encouraged to do so, she could easily feel the tension in her shoulders and neck rise in proportion to how much she exerted herself mentally on either side of her dieting issues: either focusing on dieting, or thinking she might just as well go ahead and overeat.*

- *She rolled her neck and shoulders whenever she felt tension.*

- *Regularly she asked herself what else she thought or felt when either a pro-dieting or anti-dieting thought occurred to her.*

- *She could also feel how the tension subsided when she confronted both sides of the issue.*

- *There often was a connection between the physical movements and finding that she could think things through more to her satisfaction.*

The Journey

Liz still struggled with food, but she found herself more easily dealing with her food urges. "I'll have just a few M&M's instead of a whole bag. And there are days I really enjoy just eating lightly and well. I am losing weight steadily without the struggle I had over it before." Each day she would acknowledge her ambivalence. To diet or not to diet. To overeat in response to emotional pain or not to overeat. Being more aware of opposing attitudes and feelings made following the better course easier.

Physical and Spiritual Exercise

Purpose: To relax and keep you aware of your ambivalence.

Step #1: Feel your ambivalence

- Interpret neck and shoulder tension (in part) as ambivalence.

- Roll your shoulders around—like swimming the crawl, breaststroke, or back stroke—three times in one direction, and then three times in the other direction.

- Roll your head clockwise, following your nose as if it is attached to a line pulling it around three times, and then roll in the opposite direction three times.

Continued

Step #2: Take Action

- Bring to mind any decision ahead of you. Roll your head and shoulders to physically invite your feelings into discussion of the decision you are considering.

- Think about the pros and cons of your decision. Write them out if it's something that has been an issue for a while.

- Pay attention to both your thoughts and your feelings, and notice where they oppose one another and where they agree with one another.

Step #3: Stop thinking

- Roll your shoulders and neck for 20-60 seconds, and just breathe, concentrating on just the feelings in your shoulders and neck.

Step #4: Intend to move forward

- Pick out any helpful or guiding or otherwise positive thoughts that have come to you.

- Write those on a note card or in a journal or just make a mental note.

- Roll your head and shoulders again, and "tell" yourself to keep processing the matter for you, unconsciously. The physical movement of ambivalence (shoulder and head rolling) will keep the "conversation" going between your head and your heart.

❖ STORY: Alienation and Friendship

Jim had a long history of social anxiety and an equally long history of trying just one new social thing and then stopping. Finally, confronted on his lack of progress, he decided to "really go for it and 'live life to the fullest'. I'm done playing games with you and myself about wanting to do things, and wanting to be normal, and then not doing anything. I'm going to do what I think of and stop making excuses."

Treatment

- ○ *Jim's neck and shoulders were extremely stiff and visibly rigid, apparently in direct proportion to how much effort he exerted in resisting his own thoughts and impulses toward more social connection.*

- ○ *Rolling his shoulders or neck was extremely difficult and painful, so Jim rolled slowly.*

- ○ *He read out loud daily affirmations from Dr. Susan Jeffers' book, "Feel the Fear and Do It Anyway."*

- ○ *Jim noticed how his stiffness would loosen up for a while after he pushed himself to go forward with something he wanted to do.*

- ○ *He began to notice how stiff he would feel when he avoided something he knew he should be doing.*

- ○ *The more social risks he took, the more relaxed his shoulders and neck became.*

The progress

Jim started to jump on every forward moving thought he had. He had more and more satisfying interactions, and found himself at last in the first real friendship he had experienced since childhood. To keep himself on track, he wrote or called in between sessions to report on what he was doing. In a couple of months he asked, "Why is it so much easier to roll my head and shoulders than it was when we started?" It seemed that the answer was in his acceptance of his own ambivalence, in keeping his head and heart talking to one another so he could honestly follow through on his plans, rather than get ambushed by negativity he couldn't acknowledge within himself.

Remember

Perhaps in the past you thought that having mixed feelings about something held you back from making a decision. This chapter shows you that just the opposite is true. The super-transformer of ambivalence helps you work with your contradictory thoughts and feelings and is an essential part of every well-informed decision. You will become a better decision-maker by learning to admit and feel your way through the resistance of contradictory feelings and thoughts.

Celebrate !!

* ❋ Helpful new thoughts that come your way.

* ❋ Feeling more balanced in the pace at which you deal with challenges.

* ❋ Greater ability to pursue and resolve what you want.

* ❋ Finding yourself with better timing throughout your daily activities.

CHAPTER 4

Hostility-Stress: Nuclear Power or Atom Bomb

Dr. Sharon Says

Anything worth changing is
worth getting mad about:
passionate mad, crazy mad,
angry mad, and creative mad.

When stressed or mad,
your marksmanship is awful.

Madness and stress must be activated
in order to get to the pains that created them.

As the movie title said, "It's a Mad, Mad, Mad, Mad World" and the truth is, that's not a bad thing

- **Some things are meant to be maddening** (hostility creating). It's right when injustices make you mad. It's right when you feel mad because you can't get something

right no matter how hard you try. It's maddening when something bothers you and you can't make it stop.

- **Hostility is a mixture of angers** directed outward. It's a maddening, crazy, complex mixed variety of angers that tries to make you go in too many directions all at once.

- **Acting out of hostility** is like trying to hit a golf ball 100 yards away with buckshot. First, you probably won't hit the golf ball. You'll think that you're just mad at whatever provokes your hostility, but there will be much more to it than that. Hostility tells you so. Second, you'll probably hit a lot of other stuff. There's always collateral damage when we act out of hostility, whether we are aware of our hostility or unaware. And that is even more maddening. And stressful, too.

- **Respecting your hostile feelings** involves "detonating" them safely, and then searching through the newly unearthed information: i.e., admitting your hostility, learning from it, and doing no harm.

Hostility and stress are opposite sides of the same coin

They are both the feeling of strong internal pressures going several different directions at once.

- **When you feel hostile**, you aim that pressure at something or someone, whether actually or in your words or imagination.

- **When you feel stressed**, you hold the pressure in, essentially aiming it at yourself, so as not to aim it at someone or something.

- **Experiences of hostility:** Hating someone or some thing; feeling explosive; communicating with condescension or arrogance; losing one's temper; pissed off; road rage; vindictiveness or revenge, wanting to 'get even' ; acting mad by ignoring, avoiding, cold-shouldering.

- **Experiences of stress**: Overwhelmed; upset; chronic unhappiness or frequent fearfulness; physical pain or ailments; wanting to avoid the stressful topic.

- **Sneaky signs of hostility/stress:** Offending people; withdrawal; silent when offended. Using negative judgmental words: stupid, dumb, ridiculous, obnoxious, asshole, bitch, lowlife, bastard, fuck off!, shit, etc. etc..

The high costs of unresolved hostility and stress

- When you act out your hostility on others, you have poor marksmanship. Which in turn causes backlash. Collateral damage both to yourself and others. Your points are less well taken and you make others less likely to share information with you.

- When you endure stress without letting loose, your body takes the hit and eventually the damage. If your suppressed hostility does emerge, it's with passive aggression—which is just as difficult to decipher as overt aggression—in "innocent" digs, uncooperativeness, forgetting and procrastination.

The incompleteness of "destressing" through yoga, breathing and meditation

- When you feel hostile there's good reason, even if it's only your own misconceptions.

- When you 'deep breathe' your way out of the anger or stress, there's a high probability that you are losing at least some of the information held in your hostile emotions.

The Challenge

- Rejection of hostility and ignorance that stress is related to hostility are bad for society. Both hostility and stress contain huge constructive potential.

- Just like raw atomic energy, neither can be used safely unless one knows they're there and knows how to handle them.

- In everyone, hostility needs softened, more accurate conscious expression.

- In everyone, stress needs more awareness of the hostility within.

Learning to play with hostility (and stress masking hostility) is the balanced way out of pressure

- Hostility play is the art of releasing internal pressure (i.e. blowing off steam) while being sure not to direct it at anything other than objects ready for recycling.

- Hostility play makes it possible to get to other emotions and thoughts so you can move beyond the hostility and become more accurate about what you are thinking, feeling, and needing to do.

- People often smile, laugh, or feel lighter and happier when they indulge in safe hostility play. Many times people cry, sob or simply become deeply sad as they get emotionally closer to the originating pain and need underneath their hostility and stress. Mastery of your hostility is a win-win for you and everyone around you.

❖ STORY: Weight Gain-Loss, continued:

Liz was chronically stressed by her depression, lack of control of her economic situation and difficult relationships. As soon as she felt stress, she would blame her fat. That would provoke overeating, which in turn would provide momentary relief that would later only make her feel worse, and more depressed.

Treatment

Confronted with how mean she was being to herself when stressed and depressed, Liz could easily see that what she had thought was just depression was also feeling mad at herself. As often as she could, when angry thoughts at her fat came to mind, Liz did hostility play.

- *When she caught herself blaming her fat, Liz tore up magazines she had waiting for her expression of hostility.*

- *She even kept some in the car, so frequent was her habit of being mean to herself when depressed.*

o *She got mad and did madness play to express her-self instead of trying to fight how mad she felt. She had already been mad for a long time, although it hadn't seemed so to her.*

o *She found all kinds of mad feelings. Mad at herself. Mad at others. For all kinds of different reasons.*

o *Each time she did hostility play, she found "My stress level goes down, and I can go on thinking and dealing with my day."*

Progress

Using these new tools Liz found a way out of the constant cycle of stress, depression and overeating. She began to actually have fun with her feelings. She soon found herself depressed much less often, for shorter periods of time. She also was less hungry, ate less and continued to lose weight.

Physical and Spiritual Exercise

Purpose: Relieve Stress. Clear Mind and Body for Further Thought.

Get Prepared for Extreme Hostility Play

- **When you're extremely** hostile or extremely stressed, you feel mad whether you admit it or not. Playing with such madness involves pairing irrational, mean, nasty, blaming, attacking thoughts with safe activity that involves destruction.

- **Think of anything that is stressing you or driving you nuts.**

Continued

- **Say out loud or mutter under your breath** your angry, bitter, raging, irrational thoughts while you also...

  o **Draw and immediately scribble out** stick figures, or symbols representing the offending person(s) or situation(s).

  o **Destroy something ready for recycling**: Use an old magazine or junk mail or anything else ready for the trash can.

  o **Rip the item(s) to pieces** and throw them in the trash.

  o **OR hold an expendable pen** in your fist (like you are going to stab the paper) and start scribbling HARD through the layers of a stack of old magazines (maybe tear off the covers first and rip them into itty, bitty pieces). Speak your venom out loud or muttering under your breath.

  o **Bonus:** When using the magazine scribbling method remove all the torn pages. Look at the un-torn page. Sometimes your glance falls upon an image or phrase which adds amusement or perspective to your issue.

- **Adults and children** alike can easily use the de-stressing activity of hostility (madness) play.

❖ STORY: A Man Fantasizing About Murdering His Wife

Ray couldn't stop having thoughts of murdering his wife by throwing her in front of a subway train. Prior counseling in thought stopping and positive thinking had only increased the frequency of his murderous fantasies. The thing was, he loved his wife. He didn't feel anything more than a little put upon by her at times and couldn't for the life of him figure out why he had such thoughts. Besides, where he lived there were no subways.

Treatment

Instead of fleeing from his homicidal thinking, Ray was encouraged to embellish the awful fantasy through this process:

- ○ *Eyes closed, he envisioned the murder in gory detail: imagining the fury, the deed, the blood, the death.*

- ○ *In his mind's eye he watched and then reported all the follow-up details: the arrest, the prison, the sense of loss setting in.*

- ○ *Eyes open he talked about the minor, even trivial, irritations in his life.*

- ○ *It turned out that he really was mad at the number of rude customers in his business, although he never showed it to any of them.*

Outcome

He realized that his violent fantasies contained all the unused, accumulated anger from his workdays. He became just a little less good-humored and more assertive with every nasty customer, instead of letting his antagonism build up. He also became a little more assertive with his wife on the few points where he disagreed with her. The homicidal fantasies vanished.

Physical and Spiritual Exercise

Get Prepared for Moderate Hostility Play

o **Write out your mean thoughts** using as much vile language as you like and tear up the paper you've written them on (destroy the evidence).

o **Draw how mad you are** as in the boy's story below.

o **Vividly imagine an outrageous display of how mad you are** in a mad fantasy as in the man's story above. Say or murmur under your breath the words as you imagine.

o If you have someone in your life who won't take your wicked thoughts literally, share them with the expressed intention of getting past how angry/ stressed you feel, like in the man's story above.

❖ STORY: A Child's Thoughts of Suicide

Jamie's father had committed suicide, so when Jamie said that he was thinking of killing himself, his mother hastened to bring him in for treatment. Jamie didn't like being angry and he loved being helpful to his mother. They lived with some relatives, one of whom was a boy cousin close to his own age. This boy was aggravating and troublesome to everyone, especially to Jamie. But Jamie never flew off the handle at him.

Treatment

Although Jamie didn't want to feel angry he was okay with saying and drawing how he thought about his cousin.

- ○ *He drew a full page color picture of his cousin being destroyed. Although not of course by Jamie.*

- ○ *"He's in this bag and he's had his body cut off because someone thought he was a turkey. This ear was bitten off by Mike Tyson. Someone set the bag on fire."*

- ○ *Next session after that Jamie drew pretty much the same picture but in black and white.*

- ○ *In the next session the cousin was drawn as a tiny figure in the upper left corner of the page, standing next to a grenade with a tag attached to it saying "loser".*

Outcome

Jamie's suicidal thoughts disappeared. He had worked through his feelings about his cousin, his dad and himself by directing his anger into mad art and then talking about it to his psychologist. The drawings about his cousin were elegant in their message. Jamie was mad. But he didn't have to act mad at his cousin because he knew that his cousin would 'get what was coming to him' (never verbally expressed by Jamie) just because of his "loser" behavior. The drawings probably also helped Jamie resolve the much deeper issues of his anger at his father for having committed suicide, and the challenge of loving his father's memory without adopting the same suicidal or otherwise self-destructive behavior.

Remember

In this chapter you learned about both the merits and the inevitability of the super-transformer of hostility, and its relationship to stress. Exercises and case examples are designed to teach you to humor yourself through hostile, stressed or mad feelings. As you use the methods, you will discover feeling lighter, happier, and clearer in your thoughts and will find yourself more aware of and able to handle your stress and anger.

Celebrate !!

✳ Feeling lighter, happier and freer after venting hostility or stress.

✳ Being safer for others to live with.

✳ Being able to have mad / catastrophic thoughts without doing harm.

✳ Being safer for yourself instead of having to pay the costs of stress.

✳ Any laughter that comes from the relief of hostility play and/or getting perspective.

CHAPTER 5

No Pain, No Gain, Less Fun

Dr. Sharon Says

Just as a break in your skin or bone
"summons" physiological repair, so too heartbreak
and heartache summon psychological repair.

Yawning in pain gets oxygen to your tissue
and energy to your issue.

Every pain can lead to gain.
Search yourself.

Under all hostility is pain
Under all stress is pain

- You wouldn't be mad or stressed unless something was bugging you, causing you pain.

- Any chronic or large angers and stresses have a lot of pain underneath.

- Pains and their attendant stress grow with the added pain of not fixing the pain.

- Angers and hostility grow with the added pain of collateral damage from not resolving the pain.

Identifying your pain brings clarity and relief

The sooner you express the real pain underlying your hostility, stress, depression, anger, hate, lack of achievement, poor relationships, and bad habits the sooner you will heal.

- The breaking feeling of pain—as in heartbreak, skin break, bone break—acts physically and psychologically as a vacuum to suck in the help you need.

- Pain is fully effective only when it's "clean". Cleared of anger, fear, hate. Even happiness and laughter can interfere with learning from pain. Expression of clear, "clean" pain brings compassion from others, especially those who love you.

Hit The Jackpot: The great payoffs of handling your pain well

- **Makes You Grow**: When you get to the real pain (pain not entangled with other emotions) you automatically learn and grow in healthy ways.

- **Pain Stimulates Seeking of Solutions**: By its nature and physical movement—a vacuum-like sensation of breaking open—pain automatically draws in information, assistance and experience to solve the problem revealed by the pain.

- **Mastery Over Physical Pain and Addictions**: Unexpressed emotional pain is felt primarily in the stomach so it's easily confused with need for food. Out of control hungers of all kinds (including addictions) are symptoms of pain that hasn't been understood yet. Expressing the real pain helps to bypass habits that suppress the pain.

Physical Exercise

Purpose: Redirect the tension response into caring for your pain and encouraging your pain to do its healing work.

Step #1: Practice full yawning. Open your mouth wide.

Step #2: As you yawn, roll your eyes up and back under drooping eyelids, keeping your face level and not tilting your head back.

Step #3: Evaluate how much you mix yawning (pain) with other gestures (and emotions):

- o Do you tend to tilt your head back when yawning? (Laughing off your pain)

- o Is your jaw tight, making it hard to yawn? (Anger or tension at or opposition to your pain)

- o Do your eyes flit to either or both sides, or open wide? (Fearful of your pain)

Continued

Step #4: If you find yawning difficult, try the following exercise:

- **Shake yourself gently** head to toe as if feeling a tingle throughout your body.

- **Breathe in** through loosely parted lips as you gently "tremble" yourself.

- **Exhale slowly** through loosely closed lips. Let your lips puff up, and out, with your out-breath.

- **Repeat the preceding three movements** until you automatically yawn. If you don't automatically yawn, try several more cycles of gentle"trembling", loose exhaling, and yawning.

Step #5: So as not to get stuck in any emotional or physical pain or in a depressed mood:

- **Numb your pain.** Breathe in through your nose and breathe out through loosely closed, puffy lips (the "leaky tire" exhale).

- **Distract yourself from pain.** Breathe in and out through slightly parted lips and imagine a tingle throughout your body. Next tighten your abs and gently straighten up your body. Then do some activity...without focusing on your pain.

- **Welcome tears.** Seldom is pain accompanied by tears, but when they come, tears help to wash out tension more dramatically and quickly than just yawning.

- **Be sure to give your pain full attention** several times daily. Only then can it subside constructively, "knowing" you have gotten its message.

❖ STORY: Hunger Pains Transformed

Margaret, formerly bulimic and still suffering from emotional overeating, called before her next session. "I can't stop crying," she said. "I've been crying for days" (when not at work or with other people). I asked, "Is it different than other times?" "Yes. I'm not so angry, I'm just sad. I'm so lonely," she replied. "That's excellent," I said. "Yes," she said, "I feel like this is really about me, not about what others think, not about what others want. It's really about me!"

Treatment

Margaret began to question herself regularly about what she was really hungry for before turning to food to fix the hunger pang. Numerous emotional hungers became clearer.

- ○ *She was hungry for closeness with her mother. Margaret had felt lonely all her life. Trying to "suck up" to a mother whose way of showing affection to her was not what Margaret wanted. On top of it, Margaret's mother had the kind of relationship with Margaret's younger sister that Margaret hungered for.*

- ○ *She was starving for better treatment by the men in her life: her son, her brother, her father, her ex-husband. Her family and her brief marriage both operated on the assumption that women must take care of men.*

- ○ *She was aching for meaning in her life; for her own identity. She had devoted herself entirely to her children, who were now all in college or beyond. Her world felt empty.*

Outcome

Margaret began to say no to some of her children's demands, in a way both honestly pained and guilt-free. She talked earnestly with her mother who also wanted a better relationship with Margaret. She persevered more at her classes and found a better job. She found herself feeling more in control of her life than she ever had before.

Spiritual And Physical Exercise

Purpose: To improve your handling of pain

Step #1: Think of whether various pains in your life are pains over your own problems or pains over the problems of others. Think honestly of things that are a "pain in the neck" and things that are a "pain in the ass".

Step #2: Question how you react to those pains physically and emotionally.

- Do you heat up with fear? Or grow cold in resistance to fear?

- Do you become lethargic in numbness or sadness?

- Do you tense up in anger or fright?

- Do you keep happily in motion so you don't notice or think about it?

All of the above are natural reactions to pain. But all of them make processing of pain less efficient.

Continued

Spiritual and Physical Exercise, continued

Step #3: Ponder your pain

○ Wonder at how your natural reactions to pain interfere with your gaining knowledge and wisdom from pain.

○ Wonder at how you might be a better psychotherapist for your pain by listening to it, caring about it, and wondering what it's trying to tell you about what you need.

○ Write your thoughts of what bothers you, and what you want or wish for. Admit that these are important, and yawn as you do so.

❖ STORY: Husband's and Wife's Pain

Rodolpho understood completely his wife, Maria's, pain and depression (at a gut level, anyway). The problem was that she didn't. Maria would shut herself up in her room and try to figure things out by herself. But she wouldn't handle deeper issues—only the surface ones that needed to be dealt with at the time. Moreover too many suggestions, too much sympathy, too many questions, too much desire to help from Rodolpho only irritated her.

Treatment

Rodolpho felt frustrated and helpless at not being able to make his wife's pain go away. "I'm a Mr. Fix-it kind of guy," he said, nodding his head ruefully.

○ *"Every man in love is a fix-it kind of guy," I said. "That's what Mother Nature intended. But the thing here is that fixing it involves just making it safe for her to feel her pain. Growing up in a rough* neighborhood had meant that showing her pain would have only made her a better target. Only with you was she able to let down and relax at long last."

○ "I get it," he mused. "So I fix it in time by not fixing it right away."

○ "Yes," I replied. "She needs her pain to figure things out. She needs you to make it safe to feel her pain."

Progress

○ Rodolpho became much more patient with Maria's problems. He realized that her self-understanding was as much a part of the eventual solution as his efforts on her behalf. He asked and pushed less and was careful to ask questions that helped her.

○ With this change in Rodolpho's approach, Maria in turn found that not only could she get clarity on immediate issues more quickly, but also she began to feel more able to bring up other related issues to her husband.

Remember

Much pain highly relevant to personal improvement is lost to consciousness because, frankly, there's just so much of it. This chapter explained how to manage pain. How to invite your pain to talk to you. How to learn from it. How to take a break from it. The super-transformer of pain automatically causes learning and growth if you keep from tensing up in opposition. If you keep your mind and heart open. Find your life less burdened, less bothered, and more motivated through knowing your pain and allowing its gain.

Celebrate !!

✻ Being empowered to recognize and fix things that are bothering you.

✻ Feeling better understood by people you care about.

✻ Understanding others' problems better.

✻ Getting more of what you truly want.

CHAPTER 6

When You Hate Don't Devastate; Excavate

Dr. Sharon Says

Hate tells of need
for waste management.

Hate is an inevitable
side effect of life and love
just as poop is an inevitable
side effect of food and water.

Hate—or any other kind of waste—
in and of itself is not bad.

It's what you do with waste that
can lead either to new growth
(as in proper disposal and recycling of waste)
or to damage and decay (as in pollution).

Rational (good) hate is focused on situations rather than individuals, groups, things or places

It's rational to hate situations that are bad for you.

It's healthy to feel an "ick!" or "yuck!" toward counterproductive, unhealthy habits, bad situations, disturbing patterns, and things that are just plain wrong.

Irrational (bad) hate (bitterness) = rational hate plus helplessness

When you hate a situation that's bad for you but you're helpless to do anything about it, irrational hate (bitterness) automatically takes over your body. Whether you perceive it, believe it, or not.

- The toxicity of hating the situation builds up because you're helpless to get rid of the problem.

- In your helplessness to correct the problem you will hate or be bitter toward yourself or someone or something else around you.

- Helplessness plus rational hate is at the root of all bigotry and hate crime.

Thought Tip: Prejudice and bigotry are in large measure bitterness about specific wrongs close to home being displaced onto some large out-group for "safe" avoidance of experiencing the bitterness in the in-group.

Where there is bitterness, there is also rational hate

- Your mother may have told you: "You don't hate so-and-so. You just don't like what they're doing." If so, she was trying to get you to be rational about your hate and move you out of bitterness and into the possibility of forgiveness.

- When you don't like (i.e., hate or at least sorta hate something about) someone or something you have the opportunity to clarify specific things that are keeping you helpless, including your own lack of limit-setting skill, your own nervous or cynical expectations or behaviors, and any other interfering habits that you haven't yet clarified for yourself.

Where there is bitterness helplessness awaits its chance to evolve

- When you hate yourself or someone else you are feeling helpless to choose what is good for you. Helpless at keeping good boundaries against what is bad for you.

- You are also probably much less helpless than you think. Reflect on why you have felt helpless. Very likely it's a pattern that began when you were young and truly helpless. Think of how you can get things out of the way now. You're more powerful than you were as a child.

Handling your hate well has huge payoffs

- **Improve your physical health**. Hate is your detector for things that are wrong. Ignoring it means ignoring things that literally are going to make you sick (physically, mentally, or spiritually) in time.

- **Become a better person**. Identifying rational hate will help you strip away your bigotries, prejudices, irrational biases and unfair opinions.

- **Feel more relaxed toward yourself and everyone around you**. You'll be better able to see the big picture and the different sides of issues rather than have your vision obstructed by non-recycled garbage.

Physical Exercise

Purpose: To promote physical well being.

Step #1: Recognize any nauseous, icky or distasteful sensation as the emotion of hate (not just a bad meal, the flu or too much coffee).

Step #2: Practice being aware when your tongue touches your lower lip or pushes inside your mouth into your lower cheeks. (The gestures signal not liking, or hating something and rightly resisting "swallowing" whatever it is).

Step #3: Notice when other people's tongues touch or pass their lower lips or push downward into their cheeks and behind their lower lip.

Continued

Step #4: When you feel that something is gross, disgusting, despicable, or icky, or you think it is just plain wrong, practice physically by sticking your tongue forward past your lower teeth and/or lips "…(which is not just resisting taking in something bad, but also starting to get rid of something bad you've already taken in).

Step #5: Practice the full expression of hate by touching your tongue to your chin. This is actually part of the cleansing "lion" posture in yoga. (Wet chin afterward? Of course: hate is messy.)

❖ STORY: Weight Gain-Loss, concluded

At first Liz was consumed by irrational hatred (bitterness) toward herself.

- ○ *Hating herself for being fat. Hating her fat, and feeling helpless to win against it.*

- ○ *Hating herself for being stupid. Hating that she had difficulty in school and feeling helpless to understand some of the material.*

- ○ *Hating herself for being ugly. Hating that she didn't have a healthy relationship with a man and feeling helplessly low in her self-esteem.*

Treatment

Reapplying her hate: After playing with her bitterness instead of stressing, Liz had a better grip on her hate. She could redirect it toward situations rather than at herself. Her hatred of situations became empowering because she now took hate as a sign that something truly was wrong. That it was both wrong for her and unhealthy for others around her.

o   *She focused her hate on her bad habits instead of on herself.*

o   *She realized she was "lying to myself, telling myself there's something wrong with me." She decided to hate her toxic self-statements (e.g., "I'm stupid." "I'm ugly." "I'm a fat cow.") and to treat them as garbage instead of being hateful toward herself.*

o   *She practiced improved "antidote" statements, e.g., "I'm learning to learn." "Plenty of men find me attractive. I'm just not ready yet." "My fat has been my friend. But I'm getting more and more ready to take care of myself instead of having my fat do the job."*

o   *The physical sensations of hate often continued even through the positive statements. This was the needed physical activity to eliminate the bad habits and bad patterns. The physical often takes a while to catch up with the mind when habits have been deeply ingrained.*

o   *Getting control and clarity about what she hated immediately lifted her feelings of helplessness.*

The end of treatment
For the first time in her life Liz began to truly feel like a good person. She felt her own self-worth and was able to sort things out and get back to those who upset her with excellent results. Her children, her family, teachers, her employer, friends: everyone began responding better to her.

Mental Exercise

Purpose: To admit irrational hate and use it to gain clarity

Step #1: Think of how putting up with something that is wrong for you—either because it's actually wrong or because your attitude is wrong—is literally bitter for your body and spirit.

Step #2: Question your assumptions

- When you don't like something or someone, what is really going on? What situation and what helplessness on your part are involved?

- When you "can't stand" something, what are you thinking is hateful? Is it that, or something else?

- When you "don't like" something, wonder what exactly is wrong. Don't talk yourself out of the hate. If something is wrong for you, it's wrong for all involved, because any wrong unsettles relationships.

Step #3: Hate Play, Hearts Work

- Write down both seemingly accurate and seemingly inaccurate statements. Let them flow out.

- Draw hearts around anything that seems objective or positive.

- Scribble through anything that seems irrational or offensive.

- Destroy the evidence (tear up, shred, etc.) or just fold and discard. For added body-mind satisfaction, you may want to poke holes in the scribbled-out areas before discarding.

Continued

Mental Exercise, continued

- Write again later on, aiming for continued improvement in accuracy. Keep working your hate to clear out its toxicity, and unearth the 'pearls in the poop'.

Step #4: Look for the hate around you

- Listen to others as they express hateful thoughts.

- Wonder what is wrong for them and what, if anything, there is for you to do about it. Recognize it and seek clarification.

- Think "Ick!" Think "Not good for me, and not good for it/him/her/them (whatever or whomever is involved in the toxic situation)."

- Wonder about any toxic-sounding statements you hear. Write them down and scribble them out. If you are so inclined, if they hang in your mind and they bother you.

❖ STORY: Father and Daughter-in-law

Harry had confided in his daughter-in-law, Lila, about a financial matter and asked that she not tell his son. He wanted to work it through on his own, he said, and would tell his son in time. But Lila felt uncomfortable with the matter Harry had disclosed and told her husband. Lila's husband then went straight to the investors his father was considering and threatened that he would "bury" them if they did the deal with his father. He warned them not to tell his father that he had been there. Of course Harry found out. He was furious at his son but even more furious at Lila for betraying his confidence.

Treatment

Harry was consumed with feelings of hatred toward his daughter-in-law. "I can't believe she went behind my back like that!" But the real issue was not Lila. It was his parenting of his son. He had spoiled his son financially all his life yet regularly hated his son's consequent financial irresponsibility and impulsivity.

○ *Harry planned to begin withholding some financial gifts from his son and focused his hate on his pattern of overindulging his son.*

○ *He gradually saw that he had placed Lila in an untenable position by enjoining her not to tell. He admitted that she was actually being a good wife in sharing with her husband. He focused the hate instead on his displacement of his helplessness and unhappiness over his son onto Lila.*

○ *"Well," he said, "I used the wrong words. I don't hate her. I just don't trust her."*

○ *This led to a fruitful exploration of his own helplessness due to his blind trust.*

○ *Looking back on his helplessness in situations he hated regarding his son and finances Harry began to see his son's manipulation and his own enabling responses.*

○ *Similarly, Harry began to realize that it was incumbent upon him to develop more mature self-trust and good judgment. Everything in his approach to others needed growth, from sharing money to sharing confidences.*

❖ STORY: A Happy Beginning

This time Harry refrained from staying hostile to his son and daughter-in-law for an extended period of time. Empowered by a new ability he was able to treat his son and daughter-in-law kindly and set some limits on both the financial aspects and the territorial aspects of their relationship (e.g., the son could no longer drop by unannounced). Harry knew that he had a journey ahead, however, in continuing to divest himself of his old overindulgent, ill-thought-out habits.

Spiritual and Physical Exercise

Purpose: To move past bitterness into forgiveness.

Step #1: Think of how continuing to hate even though the situation is wrong is literally sickening to your body and spirit.

Step #2: Identify and clarify your helplessness.

- Think about the specifics of what you hate and list all the "I can't" statements that fit.

- Repeat the statements one by one. As you do, sit on your hands and double over as if scrunching yourself into a ball to physically express the contracting sensation of helplessness.

- Wonder why you feel helpless. How long have you felt helpless in this way, about this sort of thing? Why were you originally helpless?

Continued

- Think of how you are less helpless now. Generate ideas of what to do differently.

- Or, admit your helplessness. Gently and kindly acknowledge your limitation, for now.

Step #3: Alternate between holding onto hate (bitterness) and letting it go (forgiveness).

- Make fists in a holding on gesture and say what you hate and what you should hate.

- Spread your hands wide in a gesture of letting go and say what you are truly helpless to change, for now.

Step #4: Use hate directly to break bad patterns

- Direct the hate at the bad pattern, or at the link in your habits that goes from a rational reaction to an irrational one.

- Vividly imagine or physically express the "blech" of hate to drive the message of breaking away from a bad habit deep into your unconscious mind for processing.

Remember

Hate gets bad press but it's how hate is handled that's the problem. In this chapter you learned what's good about the super-transformer of hate, and how hate goes bad. You learned tools to help you separate out your good hate from your bad hate. Tools to help you pursue your internal and inter-personal clean-up projects more effectively. Using these methods, you will gain power in setting things right in your life that are wrong, instead of leaving them buried or making a mess or living with messes.

Celebrate !!

✳ Growth in your compassion for yourself and/or others.

✳ The wonder of being able to clarify what's wrong and then set things straight.

✳ Feeling more powerful after uprooting old helplessness that no longer applies to you.

✳ The mental and physical happiness and lightness after disposing of hated issues.

✳ The pleasure of truly knowing that which you can change and that which you must accept at least for now.

CHAPTER 7

Without Confusion There's No New Conclusion

Dr. Sharon Says

Use your confusions for better conclusions.

Shaking your head gently in confusion
clears out cobwebs
and improves brain circulation.

Activate your confusions
to help prevent brain contusions.

Confusion is the simplest of the incredibly transforming feelings

- Simply cerebral: not head to toe.
- Won't make you DO anything.
- Automatically opens your mind when you embrace it.

Confusion is also the most immediately freeing in its effects

- **Learn New Approaches**: Confusion shakes up your expectations and perceptions so you can learn new approaches and new perspectives.

- **Get Un-Stuck on a Difficult Issue:** Just admitting that something is confusing will propel your unconscious mind to work on forming new ideas. Shaking your head in confusion will accelerate the process. Intending to gain clarity once your (conscious and unconscious) confusion has run its course will improve the results.

- **Confusion is a Core Tool** of Psychological Treatment. Patients pour out their stories and the psychologist picks out confusingly contradictory pieces of the story to juxtapose against one another for the patient to look at, question and resolve. You can do this for yourself by letting thoughts enter your mind without trying to make them fit. That forces your unconscious mind to find a broader, better thought than the contradictory ones you've been accepting.

- **The Confusion Technique** is a Major Part of Hypnotic Treatment: The psychologist using hypnosis throws in contradictory images or non-sequiturs (statements that make no logical sense based on the preceding statement). Then new thoughts are more easily inserted, as long as they fit well for the patient. You can do this for yourself by staying confused and then asking others for their views on the subject confusing you.

Stay at least a little confused even when you get answers to questions that have been bothering you. This opens you up to even more new and improved ways of thinking.

❖ STORY: Concerned Mother

More than any single issue in her life Sarah was upset and confused about her older son. "I spoiled him. He had so much talent. Everyone was in awe of him when he was in high school. But I never made him do his chores. I never denied him money. I did too much for him and I under-mined his motivation totally. And I still won't let him grow up! I know I should make him pay rent at his age, but I just can't.

Treatment

Sarah saw the patterns she had in the past with her fam-ily—her dad dominating dinner table conversation, her mother doing all the household chores while dad kicked back over billiards in the evening. Her brother indulged but not her. Yet, the same patterns were there with her parent-ing. "I feel like whatever I do for him, it isn't enough even though I intellectually know that it's more than enough!"

- o *She was seriously confused. Shaking her head at times felt like the only right thing to do as she had no idea what else to do or how else to act since her habits were so ingrained.*

- o *It was confusing that she could see the changes, know them, experience them with others, but that with her son and daughter she would feel plunged back in time.*

- o *After days of just living with her confusion whenev-er her parenting issues came up, she suddenly was able to speak to her son about what she needed from him. It came out smoothly, non-judgmentally, not angry, just strong and clear. And he responded beautifully.*

Outcome

As Sarah reflected on her adulthood she realized that she had made huge changes even before seeking treatment. Her father was now a true friend, and her brother treated her with respect. She was just clinging to old bitterness, when all was said and done, a bitterness easily triggered by her son when he behaved in ways that resembled how she had been treated growing up. Now, equally easily, she could use her confusion to get past her hair-trigger reactions.

Physical Exercise

Purpose: Optimize cerebral blood flow. Disrupt outmoded perceptions and expectations.

Step #1: Recognize that any upper head/forehead pressure and all headaches are at least partly unexpressed and unacknowledged confusion.

Step #2: Shake your head side to side while keeping your chin level. Keep your head turning back and forth slightly left-right, left-right (not too far, not too fast, not too slowly) without tipping your chin up or down. Stretch your spine up tall. Pretend a string is pulling your head skyward to make a nice, straight spindle upon which to shake your head.

Step #3: Imagine that you are shaking up the "jelly" of your brain to improve its circulation (which the gentle shaking of confusion really seems to do) and to disrupt outmoded thinking (which really does appear to happen).

Continued

> **Step #4: Vividly visualize** internal confusion as a spindle in a washing machine swishing your neurons back and forth.
>
> **Step #5: Think "Confusion!"** Think "Energize for new ideas!"

❖ STORY: A Child Molested

Four-year-old Betty, in primary custody of her father, had been molested by her mother's boyfriend. She had disclosed this to her father, who told her mother, who immediately believed what Betty said. The boyfriend was promptly sent away by her mother. Betty began treatment with both her father and mother. Her feelings were complicated. She remembered what the boyfriend did—it was a handful of times—and was angry enough that she thought he should be punished. But she also loved him.

Treatment

Near the end of treatment as Betty was talking, she began purposefully shaking her head left-right repeatedly in response to a question I had asked. "No?" I queried, automatically assuming what we usually think when someone shakes their head.

- o *"I'm confused," she said, continuing to shake her head with determination.*

- o *It was confusing for her to love the man who had molested her, but also to be angry, upset and even ashamed of what he had done to her.*

- o *And it felt good to just be confused rather than try to figure it all out, especially being only four years old.*

- o *It seemed that moment was a turning point in her acceptance of not having him in her life: holding the truth of her love for him, and the truth of his wrong done to her: confusing, but true.*

Outcome

*Betty blossomed under her Dad's care and soon accepted
that she wouldn't see her mother's boyfriend again. She
was glad he went to jail. She didn't miss him any more,
but neither was she mad at him. She was at peace.*

Spiritual and Physical Exercise

Purpose: Optimize learning

Step #1: Embrace confusion.

- Tell yourself "It's good to be confused!" or "I can learn
  more when I admit I'm confused!" or "Confusion can
  lead me to good questions I'd never have thought of
  without it." Use the head shaking of confusion in order
  to confirm your acceptance of confusion within both your
  body and your spirit.

Step #2: Ask certain questions to keep confusion active and to
keep yourself unstuck.

- When should you pause and admit your confusion?

- Where would admitting confusion help you to be more
  real, more flexible, and better able to go with the flow?

- When you're confused, how soon should you move on
  and just ignore what's confusing you for the time being,
  in order to go with the flow on what's good or clear?

Step #3:

- Write down elements of a problem before you. Shake
  your head in confusion.

Continued

- Next write down happy parts embedded in the problem, e.g., the lessons you can learn or how much worse it could be. Shake your head in confusion over the contradictions between the burdens and the benefits.

- Make a note to yourself saying, "Remember flow. Use my confusion." Meditate on these concepts whenever you're confused.

❖ STORY: Elder's Story Post-Stroke

John was two years post stroke and, as is true for many patients after stroke, he was severely depressed. But until coming in for psychological treatment he and his daughters did not realize that it was depression plaguing him. His daughters thought he was just being lazy. John believed that it wasn't possible to regain better functioning in the ways his daughters believed he could.

Treatment

Confusion emerged as John's best friend. For most of his life he had been one to write off contradictions and confusion. Now he hung onto contradictory information (like his disbelief in progress versus his daughters' belief) and allowed himself to feel his confusion.

- ○ *When confused, having forgotten something, he would stop and shake his head.*

- ○ *When feeling overwhelmed with what to do next he would stop and shake his head.*

Results

Acceptance and use of confusion helped to lift John's depression. Regular head shaking when he found himself confused or otherwise befuddled improved his memory and organizational skills. He actually began to function at better than pre-stroke conditions, as reported by both himself and his daughters.

Remember

In this chapter you learned amazing benefits of the super-transformer of confusion for learning. Simple exercises can help you improve your memory, attention, and cognitive abilities in general. They also can help smooth social interactions by freeing you from the throes of judgmental thoughts and feelings. Find yourself more open to your life experiences and experience being happier in the flow.

Celebrate !!

❊ Improving your memory.

❊ Being able to come up with new approaches to old problems.

❊ Being able to fix your thoughts, attitudes and behavior more easily.

❊ Easily putting things that are bogging you down on a back burner.

❊ The joy of staying more in touch with the good things in life.

CHAPTER 8

Guided Shame Improves Your Aim.

Dr. Sharon Says

When there is blame on either side,
there is shame on both sides.

After you hunch and hide in shame
you can straighten up and improve your aim.

Beware of blame
when you process your shame.

The challenge of shame is that
its social actions of hiding
also can hide the shame.

Shame is the main emotion driving success

- Shame is the reason we take responsibility for our actions.
- Shame is what governs all social conventions.

- Without shame we would take what we wanted without thought of another. We'd invade where we wanted without respect for the boundaries of another.

Shame tells you when you've broken an important rule

- Healthy shame is about healthy behavior at your level of potential ability within your social group.

- Toxic shame is about unhealthy expectations learned within a group.

- Teenagers behave badly in part out of toxic shame at not fitting in with unhealthy standards of their peer group.

- Shame governs huge amounts of routine social behavior. Wearing of clothing is partly driven by shame. So is breaking eye contact during conversation rather than staring. Lying to mask deviations from social expectations is laced with shame.

- Men automatically feel shame when they fail to please and protect the woman they love.

Shame is the flip side of blame

- When someone feels ashamed in their intimate relationship, both partners share equally in the shame.

- When someone blames their mate, both partners are equally to blame.

- Both shame and blame, on both sides, are needed to improve a relationship.

- Getting stuck in shame can distract a person from benefiting from their need to blame.

- Getting stuck in blame can keep a person from recognizing their own shame.

Lack of access to the full power of shame leads to many problems

- When we blame someone else or ourselves for something, it is easy to fail to recognize and utilize the shame that is ALWAYS there...somewhere. Failing that, we stay stuck.

- Stuck without our shame, we fail to benefit from shame's incredible power to help us readjust in the right direction.

Shame is your healthy kick in the pants.

Healthy shame isn't about knowing the right thing to do. It's about doing the best possible thing immediately even if you are clueless as to why you have been behaving in shameful ways.

- Shame is about taking some kind of constructive action even if you don't "get" what's wrong now.

- Recognition of your shame keeps you from lolling around in shameless defensiveness, self-justification or self-satisfaction.

- Whether your shame seems fair or unfair, "toxic" or healthy, you must work with it in order to successfully achieve a better outcome.

- Molested children and rape victims rightly feel shame, even though "participation" in the criminal sexual behavior was entirely out of their control. Bringing that shame to the surface of their consciousness helps them break the cycle of helplessness and blame.

Even toxic shame is a healthy kick in the pants

- Realizing that you feel ashamed about something that you should feel good about is a clear signal to get to the bottom of your toxic shame.

- Only wading through toxic shame will remove it once and for all.

❖ STORY: Sexy Big Women

Amy felt ashamed of her large size and what she considered to be her physical unattractiveness. But when her sister Rita joined her in treatment, Amy's shame shifted. Rita was just as large as Amy and always had a never-ending flow of men at her beckon and call.

Treatment

Amy began to think that her size was not the problem after all. Then her shame turned in a healthy direction.

- ○ *She decided that she needed to truly believe that she could be big and sexy.*

- ○ *Amy shamed herself for thinking awful, mean, and/or untrue thoughts about how her fat made her un-sexy.*

○ *She strengthened her physical and mental self-shaming saying "The devil tells lies", referring to her habits of defeatist thinking.*

Outcome

Amy started feeling more confident about men, enjoying dating more than she ever had before. She was amazed to find, as her sister always knew, that there were plenty of fine men who liked "big".

Physical Exercise

Purpose: To help you feel the positive power of shame

Step #1: Feel how shame can be expressed by hiding of any kind.

- Hiding information (lying, forgetting to tell, leaving out important information)

- Hiding out instead of socializing (social withdrawal, social discomfort)

- Avoiding eye contact (including wearing hats or hoods to cover the face)

Step #2: Divert your indirect expressions of shame into direct expressions. Fully express shame physically by...

- Hunching your shoulders up, up, up to your ears, and ...

- Burying your face in your hands, and ...

- Keeping your eyes and mouth at least partly open.

Step #3: Practice physical expression of shame when...

- You violate any of your own standards.

Continued

Physical Exercise, continued

- You behave in a way that you'd be embarrassed or defensive about if the entire world could see it.

- You behave in ways that others think are shameful or embarrassing, even if you disagree.

NOTE: Shame is the one emotion that is critical to express physically for optimum effectiveness. This may be because shame's effect is so simple and direct when experienced in its pure emotional form, but is so utterly obscured and diluted if experienced in its multiple social forms of hiding, lying, and self-deception.

❖ STORY: An Unhappy Husband

Sam had always lost his temper easily. Now with his daughter a challenging teenager and his wife absorbed in activities for their two young sons, he had a shorter fuse than ever. He felt he didn't matter to his wife and kids. That all he was good for was earning a living and doing chores around the house. Jane didn't understand why Sam was so negative about their marriage and why he exploded so often. She tried to please him in many ways, but the ways she expressed her love weren't hitting Sam's radar. He wanted to be treated kindly. He wanted a hug or kiss now and then. Sam didn't understand how Jane didn't hold grudges (unlike him), and how she could love him if she didn't show her love the way he expected.

Treatment

Both Sam and Jane took responsibility for not meeting their partner in ways meaningful to him/her.

- ○ *When blaming each other had brought out enough of the issues, each turned to self shame.*

- ○ *Sam shamed himself for being stubborn and losing his temper.*

- ○ *Jane shamed herself for sticking to an old assumption that she could just punch Sam when she was joking, and never show tenderness.*

- ○ *Sam shamed himself for going too far with teasing.*

- ○ *Jane shamed herself for keeping up a wall of distrust and coldness and never giving Sam a chance.*

Outcome

Their mutually blaming stand-off softened in response to their self-shaming. Once they accepted that they had both been naughty, each in their own way, it was easier to change. Jane became more tender towards Sam. Sam gave up behaviors that truly annoyed the otherwise tolerant Jane.

Spiritual Exercise

Purpose: To help you apply the positive power of shame

Step #1: Create and repeat daily positive statements about shame.

- "Yeah. I should be ashamed (about anything where you fall short of your goals, or keep doing something counterproductive or just plain wrong)."

- "I am a good person to feel ashamed. It shows I care."

Continued

Spiritual Exercise, continued

- "My shame gives me the leg up (kick in the pants) to go where I need to go."

Step #2: Use good questions to search for what exactly it is that you can change.

"How can I do this better?"

"How does this need improvement?"

"Where do I need to apply my efforts?"

"Where can I turn for help?"

Step #3: Ask yourself about your issues with success and failure.

"What am I afraid to do my best on?"

"How do I sabotage myself?"

"What am I afraid to not do well on?"

"Where (how) do I give up before beginning?"

❖ STORY: Terrified father, cruel child

A father was terrified that his six-year-old son was on the road to becoming a mass murderer. Seriously. For two years now, the boy seemed to have no empathy for others and no remorse for misbehavior. He would spin the wheels on a bicycle and try to get his two- and four-year-old brothers to stick their fingers in the spokes. He would try to get them to jump down from heights that he wouldn't. When they were hurt, he showed neither sympathy nor regret. When he was punished, he would just look away. To his parents it seemed he was never sorry.

Treatment

Mother and father came with their son to treatment. The history was normal except for a fire that had leapt out of the wall in a room where the boy was with his mother when he was four years old. When this incident was mentioned the boy became nervous (legs swinging). The sudden surge of fear in the child suggested that he was still traumatized by the fire.

- o *In session the parents were asked to sit close together and hold their son on both their laps.*

- o *We then pretended two scenarios in vivid replay: 1) that the fire was happening, and 2) that the nightmares were happening.*

- o *For both scenarios the parents shook themselves and their son. Shaking from head to toe, saying how scary it was, and how scary it would be if it ever happened again.*

The parents had unwittingly created toxic shame over their son's fear. Their well-intentioned assurances had come across to him as telling him he was wrong to be afraid. He had become numb not only to his fear, but also to his sadness. Instead of feeling his own feelings, he would put his little brothers in dangerous, hurtful situations, and watch the feelings in his brothers rather than experience them himself.

- o *In parting they were told that when the little boy looked away upon being chastised they were to say "Oh, I can see that you are ashamed of what you did. That shows what a good boy you are."*

Outcome

All misbehaviors of the little boy vanished, permanently, before the second session. When there are no complicating factors, rapid results like this are frequent among children under age seven because they are easily hypnotized (or "entranced"). Thus they can much more easily re-experience a trauma, and subsequent rescue and relief.

Remember

Shame seems a bad thing to many people but in fact the super-transformer of shame is the core of what keeps people good. Learn to identify and work with shame, to actively invite it to help you step up to challenges confronting you. If you master the emotion of shame you will become better at identifying what holds you back, better at creating pathways to success in every area you care about.

Celebrate !!

※ Your innate goodness when you feel ashamed of anything.

※ When you use shame to boot yourself into behaving better.

※ Shame's remarkable effectiveness in getting you focused on the right path to the kind of success you need.

※ How shame helps you get along better with others.

※ More successes in every part of your life.

CHAPTER 9

Joy and Pain Improve You and Their Bonus is Laughter

Dr. Sharon Says

Pain can be maddening
and that's a good thing.

Without laughter there is only madness.
But without madness there is less laughter.

Life is a mad, glad journey.

Pain begins and joy ends.
Laughter connects them.

Pain and joy are the emotions of
beginning, completion, and beginning again.
Laughter bubbles up in the moment of union.

Joy and pain are virtues.

"God has told us to be joyful even when our hearts lie panting on the floor." ("Fiddler on the Roof," lyrics by Sheldon Harnick)

"Rejoice." (Psalms)

"Parting is such sweet sorrow."
("Romeo and Juliet," by William Shakespeare)

"No pain, no gain." (Athletic coaches everywhere)

"The more we laugh, the more we fill with glee. The more the glee, the more we're a merrier we."
("I Love to Laugh" from "Mary Poppins", lyrics by Richard M. Sherman and Robert B. Sherman)

Joy and pain breathe life into the other five super-transforming feelings

There is joy in knowing...

- ❖ Shame—so you can learn where you haven't known how to measure up, instead of falling short.

- ❖ Confusion—so you disrupt old, unimproved ideas.

- ❖ Hate—so you can identify the wrong you need to correct, and eliminate bad habits.

- ❖ Ambivalence—so you can keep your head and heart working together on decisions.

- ❖ Hostility—for the power to blow yourself out of being stuck.

There is healthy, helpful pain in feeling...

⌘ Shame—so you care honestly and productively from not doing as well as you can.

⌘ Confusion—so that you can notice accurately enough to find new, improved ideas.

⌘ Hate—so you want to correct what's wrong.

⌘ Ambivalence—so you care about what both your head and heart have to say.

⌘ Hostility—so you can figure out what's bugging you.

Joy and pain fully expressed are meant to lead to the laughter of full engagement in life

⌘ The sweetness of honest shame in fully admitting naughty behavior or thoughts is funny.

⌘ The simplicity of full confusion is funny in the face of the complexity of change.

⌘ The highly effective purgative action of hate is funny in the face of how true it is...but mostly not.

⌘ Ambivalence is funny in its humbly quiet place of decision suspended between arguing points of view.

⌘ Hostility is funny when it's detonated safely, when you and others know you do but don't mean it, and when you find truth in the ashes.

❖ STORY: Lovers as healers

Larry and Nina had reached a deep moment in their session. Larry was quietly talking, his pain poignant and clear, about how he had never felt he could please his father although they had been close before Larry became a teen. Nina was listening intently, tears in her eyes, feeling for him, as Larry shrugged in resignation, saying that he probably would never be good enough in his father's eyes.

Treatment:

I turned to Nina to ask what she thought was log-jamming Larry's relationship with his father. Her eyes still teary but also full of joy in her love, she looked understandingly at Larry. She said she thought his father had become jealous of Larry in Larry's teen years. As she explained why she thought parents become jealous of their children, and why she thought it had happened to Larry, his demeanor shifted from pessimism and despair toward doubt (a combination of confusion and ambivalence).

- ○ *I said something empathic toward the pain, for Larry, of Nina's observation being true...*

- ○ *...and paused as Larry absorbed his own emotions and Nina's words...*

- ○ *...I then I said "...suuuucckkks..." (empathizing with the rightful...even joyful...hatred of a bad situation).*

Outcome

Larry smiled with wry relief and regret and Nina burst out laughing. After the moment passed, I asked her what she found funny, and she said "You say the most unexpected things!" Indeed. Out of deeply painful misery and then into rightful—joyful—objectivity is a fully funny kind of unexpected.

Laughter IS enlightenment

Genuine laughter actually IS enlightenment. Enlightened, we understand bigger pictures of safety, beauty or balance. Laughing, we pick ourselves up from inevitable falls as we travel along our emotional roads.

- o Understanding that we are safe despite being scared is funny.

- o Understanding that we are loved despite our shameful behavior is funny.

- o Being painfully confused and yet knowing that we can still go smoothly on our way in the day is funny.

- o Being ambivalent in the face of what seems obvious is funny.

- o Feeling hate and rage and expressing them with absurd or melodramatic, yet safe, behavior is funny.

Physical Exercise

Purpose: To help you physically link agony and ecstasy into laughter.

Step #1: Practice full-bodied laughter regardless of whether something seems funny.

- Rock gently back and forth between backward circular arching of your spine and forward circular arching of your spine.

- Breathe in and out of your loosely opened, smiling mouth.

- In your backward arch stretch your chin as far upward as comfortable.

- In your forward arch stretch through the top of your head as if you are a giraffe.

- Say "ha-hah-ha-hah-ha-hah" as you rock and stretch.

- Breathe as deeply as possible, so your belly "jiggles like a bowl full of jelly" (or at least somewhat deeply and loosely).

Step #2: When you laugh, notice your mixed emotions.

- Keeping your teeth or lips together in laughter indicates tension or anger.

- Keeping your head erect instead of tilting back and upward while laughing indicates discomfort or vigilance.

- Hunching up your shoulders as you laugh suggests the presence of shame.

- Slouching your shoulders and dropping your chin on your chest indicates helplessness.

Continued

Step #3: Separate your laughter from the other emotions it's mixed with.

- Throw your head back to take a deep breath as you prepare to let loose in pure laughter.

- Double over as you exhale in full-bodied laughter.

- Stick your tongue out or think "yuck" to tell yourself to "dump" the connection that causes you to express some other emotion mixed in with laughter.

- Express the mixed-in emotion(s).

- Again rock back and forth in laughter. Notice whether your expression is more in the direction of free, full laughter.

- Wonder what the mixed-in emotion was about—the tension, vigilance, shame, helplessness, etc.—and how it became entangled with laughter.

Step #4: Practice "inviting" the full spectrum of liveliness into your expression.

- Yawn in pain.

- Jump and grin for joy.

- Throw your head back and laugh.

- Each day expect to experience pain, joy, and hearty laughter. As one spiritual master said, "If I have not cried and laughed every day, I have not truly lived every day."

Continued

Step #5: Yet another step?! Yes...it takes a lot of work to get to full, clear, laughter. So watch to see when...

- "Some people laugh through their noses
- Some people laugh through their teeth goodness sakes, hissing and fizzing like snakes
- Some laugh too fast
- Some only blast
- [Some] squeak as the squeakelers do
- [Some] let go with a ho-ho-ho-ho...
- or a ha-ha-ha-ha-ha-ha too"

["I Love to Laugh" from "Mary Poppins", lyrics by Richard M. Sherman and Robert B. Sherman]

Pain, joy and laughter are all emotional sources of prayer

- In pain we pray for help, guidance and assistance.
- In joy we pray our praise, affection, interest, awe, admiration and approval.
- In laughter we exult in the Divine Comedy of life.

❖ STORY: The Fun of Psychological Growth

An 84-year-old recently said, "I didn't know therapy was supposed to be this much fun." Indeed. I think psychological treatment should be fun because the purpose of unearthing pain is to facilitate relief, healing and return to joy... hence laughter.

Treatments and Outcomes

Certainly my aim is to make sure everyone has some form of resolution and a new door opened for change in virtually every session. But that doesn't explain how funny things get throughout sessions. My best guess is that the humor lies in the love I have for pain as well as joy, for rage as well as laughter, and the ease with which I can help people move in and out of these states.

- o *When I dryly note, "Well, you certainly wouldn't expect THAT to upset you" in response to someone thinking he shouldn't feel as he does...*

- o *Then the person bursts out in laughter with a gut-level realization that their upset makes sense.*

- o *Or when I comment with a tenderly teasing smile, "Well, just as he was overly indulged as a child and teen, you were overly trained at caretaking" ...*

- o *Then a wife stuck in the power struggle with her husband suddenly cracks up, saying "I have to laugh, or I'll cry," but suddenly cries as she feels the depth of strain from her life of caretaking, and laughs again... more softly and deeply after her tears.*

Remember that throughout growth it takes both agony and ecstasy to be fully alive.

Any time you mentally and emotionally reach beyond yourself to acknowledge connection with, or lack of connection with, and/or power over your destiny, you set yourself on the track to self-improvement.

Spiritual Exercise

Feeling joy

- Celebrate the synchronicity, serendipity and connectivity of existence: God or a Higher Power, Nature or the Universe.

- Express the "V" of victory or jump of joy over every goodness of people in your life, often: family members, friends, community members and even strangers.

- Praise in celebration often on your own in a prayerful way that acknowledges the vast interconnectedness underlying any joy you experience.

Using Joy

- Joyfully count and celebrate (with physical or mental V's of victory) your blessings daily: love, health, the beauty surrounding you, safety, and success. Whether yours personally or of people or things around you when their successes affect you positively. No matter how indirectly.

- Do the same with your affection, interest, and admiration. Spread your light near and far. Far and wide. Share joy. Show joy.

- Celebrate people in person.

- Praise and admire with letters and gifts.

- Do good deeds for yourself and others that bring you more joy.

Using pain

- When you don't feel joy at your good deeds, pray to God or petition the Universe for intention and belief that what you honestly want and need is not just for your own good, but also for the greater good.

Continued

- Write your wish to gain what you need.

- Say your purpose in learning, knowing better what you truly want.

- Pray or petition for not just what you want, but also for the wisdom to choose the right path in fulfilling it.

- When you sort of want (but lack the will) pray or petition for the will.

- Discuss your conflicts over doing good and feeling good (joy) with friends and family.

- Seek expert advice and wise counsel.

Using laughter

- Marvel at the freedom and absorb your mastery over thought, emotion and perspective.

- Feel the massage of your "innards" and soak up the sensation as one of deepened well being.

- Beam the residual lightness from your laughter both outward and inward when you are done laughing.

- Marvel at the wisdom and let your mind be boggled by the healing action of laughter.

- Laugh again. Fully.

Remember

Pain and joy are the emotions of beginning, completion, and beginning again. This chapter brings to your attention the healthy synchronicity of joy and pain. Pain underlies all needs and wants. Joy signals fulfillment and provides the energy to address and care for other pains. And as you handle your pain and realize your joy more and more effectively, your bonus is the super-transformer of laughter: the miraculous healing force that catapults you from pain into joy.

Celebrate!!

- Breathing and the joy of it.
- Being alive and the joy of beauty and rightness around you.
- Feeling the emotions—pain and joy and laughter—which add depth and power to prayer and yearning.
- Caring (which comes from pain).
- Being able to learn and grow (which comes from pain and laughter ... growing pains).
- The amazing purpose and useful function of every emotion.
- That there are no "bad" emotions: only stuck places.

Afterword

The concepts in this little book are part of a Unified Theory of Emotion which has been in development in my private practice since 1989.

The ideas and how to link them together are very much a work in progress. In fact, a long-time patient/client who looked at the manuscript exclaimed, "All these emotions are supposed to lead to joy? I didn't know that." Apologetically, I explained to her that the role of joy in relationship to the other super transformers had only crystallized in my mind a few months earlier.

I would be most grateful to hear back from you on what made sense, what confused you too much, and any questions or suggestions you have. Please feel free to e-mail me at drsharon@ surfyoursoul.com and/or check out more on the Unified Theory of Emotion at www.surfyoursoul.com.

As I said in the Introduction, I am passionate about helping people to become more fully human through truly knowing their emotions. I look forward to becoming better and better at that with your help.

Relationship Publications™

First published 2011